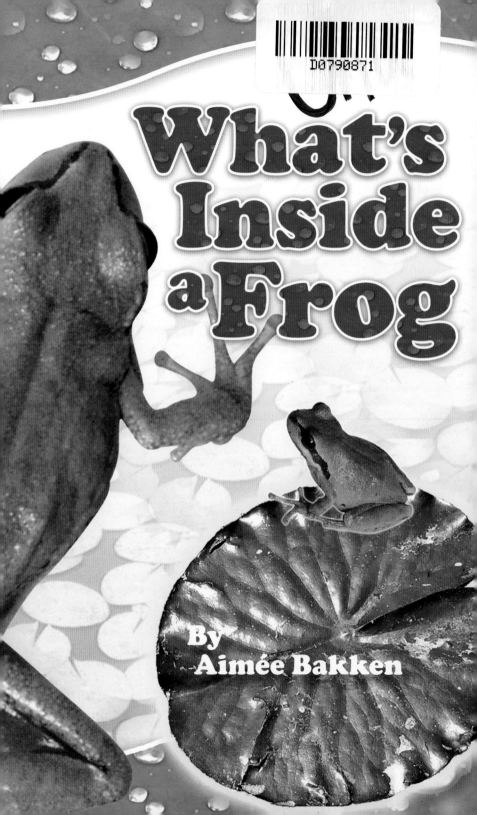

What's Inside a Frog

By
Aimée Bakken

Produced by becker&mayer!, LLC.
11010 Northup Way
Bellevue, WA 98004
www.beckermayer.com

If you have any questions or comments about this product, send email to infobm@beckermayer.com.
All rights reserved.

What's Inside a Frog is part of the Look Inside a Frog kit.
Not to be sold separately.

Edited by Don Roff
Art directed by Lisa M. Douglass
Illustrated by Davide Bonadonna and Ryan Hobson
Product design by Mark Byrnes
Product photos by Keith Megay
Production management by Blake Mitchum
Additional text by Frank M. Young

Photo credits:
Book cover/title page: Clinging frog and sitting frog © Nova Development Corporation. **Page 4:** Goliath frog © JupiterImages Corporation. **Page 5:** European tree frog; frog and toad © Nova Development Corporation. **Page 6:** Blue poison dart frog © Calvin J. Hamilton. **Page 9:** African reed frog © Nova Development Corporation. **Page 10:** Frog eggs © JupiterImages Corporation. **Page 10–11:** Tadpole © JupiterImages Corporation. **Page 12:** Coqui frog on leaf © USDA photo. Used with permission. **Page 14:** Tadpole © JupiterImages Corporation. **Page 18:** Sitting frog © Nova Development Corporation. **Page 19:** Green frog © Nova Development Corporation. **Page 20:** Frog in pond © Nova Development Corporation. **Page 24:** Leaping frog © Nova Development Corporation. **Page 25:** Frog on lily pad © Nova Development Corporation. **Page 25:** Camouflaged frog and frog on palm © Nova Development Corporation.

Printed, manufactured, and assembled in China.
10 9 8 7 6 5 4 3 2 1
ISBN: 0-439-83093-1
05224

table of contents

what is a frog?

Cuban pygmy frog

Hop! Hop! Hop! The green muscular legs rocket the European tree frog from lily pad to lily pad in the misty pond. Almost everyone knows what a frog is—but few know much more than they're green, "slimy," and they hop! But there's much more to know. Did you know that frogs have been hopping around since the time of the dinosaurs? And did you also know that there are currently over 4,000 different kinds of frogs?

Coming in all shapes and sizes—from the half-inch Cuban pygmy to the foot-long Goliath frog of western Africa—frogs belong to a group called anurans (uh-NOO-runz). Frogs live pretty much everywhere in the world—except Antarctica! So unless you live in that chilly place, chances are you've seen a frog hopping along near your home.

One if by land, two if by sea...

Frogs can go almost anywhere! Reptiles and turtles can live in water and on land—but frogs can breathe in both environments. Frogs belong to the zoological class Amphibia, meaning "both lives"—both in and out of water. There are other amphibian groups besides the anurans. *Urodeles* (YER-uh-deelz) include salamanders and newts. *Caecelians* (si-SILL-yunz) include blind, legless, wormlike animals.

Goliath frog

European tree frog

True or tree?

True frogs are the most common species. They are members of the family *Ranidae*. Tree frogs are part of the *Hylidae* family. Tree frogs have a sticky disk on each toe that helps them climb trees and shrubs. Found in tropical and temperate regions, tree frogs tend to be smaller than true frogs.

Frog or toad: who's who?

You may have wondered before, "What's the difference between a frog and a toad?" At first, it might be hard to tell. To help answer the age-old question, here are a few fun facts!

Frogs have moist, soft, smooth skin.
Frogs have long, muscular hind legs for jumping.
Frogs are brightly colored.

Toads have dry, bumpy, "warty" skin.
Toads have short hind legs for walking.
Toads have dull colors.

Frogs and toads belong to the order Anura, so toads are technically frogs.

Next time you see a frog or a toad, remember these simple rules so you can tell who's who!

the skinny on skin

Can you imagine breathing through your skin? How cool would that be? Frogs can do it! In addition to protecting the frog from the burning sun and freezing conditions, the skin is also a source of respiration. That's because their lungs alone aren't sufficient enough to supply them with their oxygen needs. Like humans, however, the frog's skin is the largest organ of the body. A frog's skin can also have distinctive colors and markings to attract mates.

Poison darts or arrows

Look, but don't touch! South America's poison dart (or poison arrow) frogs are aptly named. Their name comes from an ancient tradition. Local Indians, knowing of the frog's deadly poisons, rubbed the tips of their arrows and blow darts against its colorful skin. The poisons of the dart frog's skin can paralyze animals being hunted by the Indians. *Dendrobates*—the most well-known of poison dart frogs—are found in Central and South America. These brilliant-colored frogs—in bright hues of blue, yellow, and green—are some of the most toxic and deadly animals on Earth!

poison dart frog

Gone in sixty seconds...

It takes one minute or less for a frog's skin to change shades.

Coat, er, <u>skin</u> of many colors

Just like the shirts at your local clothing store, frogs have more than one color. They come in shades of red, blue, yellow, brown, and black. Bright colors in the skin warn would-be predators that the frog is poisonous—and not tasty. Once an attacking predator gets a mouthful of a poisonous frog, it's unlikely he will go back for a second helping! The tree frog's brilliant green color is a perfect blend of the blue pigment in the middle layer of its skin and yellow pigment from the top layer.

pumping green

Are you able to leap great distances on land and also be an accomplished swimmer in the water? Frogs can do both! On dry land frogs can walk, hop, and jump. In the water they are masterful swimmers. The secret of a frog's success is their long, muscular back legs. If you had the leg muscles of a frog—you would be able to leap over a big truck in a single bound! Frogs need strong muscles to capture food and escape from predators.

The right muscle for the job

Muscles that work against one another are called *antagonistic muscles*. Just like people, frogs have them too. When the frog's front leg muscles contract, the back ones relax, and vice versa. The frog's front and rear leg muscles develop according to how it gets around. Jumping frogs have powerful muscles in their hind legs, while the legs of a walking or swimming frog tend to be smaller.

Run silent, run deep

A frog's head doesn't move very far. Its short neck is firmly attached to

What a big head you have!
the African reed frog can inflate the
sac beneath its chin until it's bigger
than its head!

its large body. To spy what's going on around it, the frog's eyes pop up out of the water—like the periscopes of a submarine. Their eyes move in many directions, as they scan the horizon. Muscles contract in the roof of the frog's mouth to raise its eyes. These same muscles can also retract, to lower the eyes and to help them swallow. The frog also lowers its eyes to sleep. Its eyelids do not close well. When the frog's eyes are up, a *nictitating membrane* can also be lowered for protection.

A built-in cell phone

A male frog can send his mating call up to one mile away. Talk about a long distance call! What's his secret? Muscles of the trunk and the echo chambers formed by the vocal sacs give the male the ability to pump up the volume. The frog makes his call by pushing air from his lungs out, and over, the vocal cords in his throat. The frog's trunk muscles—which grow before the breeding season, when they're most needed—contract to push out the air. Some aquatic frogs use their enlarged *tympanic membranes*—the external eardrums—to further amplify their mating calls.

tastes like... frog
Frogs shed about once a week. They
pull their old skin off over their
heads in one piece and then eat it.

nictitating membrane

a frog is born

What is born in the water with gills and a tail, eventually sprouts legs, and then climbs up onto dry land? Why, a frog of course. But the life of a frog doesn't end there! When breeding season begins, they return to the water to lay eggs. Newly born tadpoles are eventually born from the eggs and the cycle begins again... and again. The circle of life, you could say.

How it begins

Where exactly does a frog come from? A female frog's ovaries contain egg cells called *oocytes* (OH-uh-sites). It takes about three months for an oocyte to grow and store the yolk. Hormones, activated by rising temperatures and the mating calls of males, move the mature eggs from the ovaries into the abdominal cavity. Then they are swept into the *cloaca*, the anus. As they move, the eggs are thickly coated with jelly.

Making frogs

eggs

During *amplexus*, where the male frog grasps ahold of the female frog to mate, the female lays her eggs into the water. The male then releases sperm from his cloaca over the eggs. The eggs are now fertilized. The frog embryos begin their development. The jelly covering swells around the eggs to keep them secure and connected. The jelly also protects the developing embryos from infection by aggressive microorganisms.

It's a fish-eat-frog world!

What are those strange-looking jelly things in the water? Clusters of developing frog embryos can be found in springtime ponds, stuck up against plants. You may have seen them. Each of these clusters could have as many as 1,000 embryos! The female must lay so many eggs because fish, and other predators, will eat most of them before they transform into adults. Many surviving young froglets will be eaten before they can start another generation. An adult frog's lifespan—up to 20 years in captivity—is only 5 to 10 years in the wild.

tadpole

male midwife

the male midwife toad attaches fertilized eggs to his hind legs. He keeps them moist. When they're ready to hatch, he returns to the water.

Speak up, pal!

During breeding season, the competition is pretty tough for the male coqui frogs of Puerto Rico. They have to croak their loudest, to be heard over the racket. They can croak as loud as 95 decibels. That's only five decibels less than a jackhammer!

coqui frog

Acidic arrest

The gastric brooding frog of Australia—a species thought to have been extinct since 1985—can stop the production of hydrochloric acid in its stomach. Why? Its tadpoles grow into frogs inside the mother's stomach! The mature froglets then hop out of her mouth.

gastric brooding frog

Losing the fat

Some frogs breed only once per year—usually in the spring. Frogs in warmer climates breed year-round. Both males and females have well-developed fat glands in their abdomens. They can use their fat supplies to live on, in case food becomes scarce. The female frog can metabolize (turn into food) the nutrients stored in her oocytes to keep going.

fat glands

just like a kangaroo!

The marsupial frog carries her fertilized eggs in a pouch just like a kangaroo! When the eggs are ready to hatch, the mother opens the pouch with her toes... and off the tadpoles swim!

blood in, blood out

What is something that you and a frog have in common? It is the circulatory system. Like a human being's circulatory system, a frog's has two parts—first, the heart pumps new, oxygen-rich to the body through vessels; next, the old, used up blood is pumped from the vessels back to the heart. So, the next time you see a frog, perhaps you have a heart-to-heart talk about the circulatory system that you share.

Tell-tale toes!

Can you imagine breathing through your toes? A frog's skin is crisscrossed with many capillaries to help it breathe. These capillaries are needed to absorb oxygen and to dispose of carbon dioxide. The capillaries are easily seen in the webbing between a frog's toes.

toe webbin

Three chambers

A frog's heart has three chambers: two *atria* and one common *ventricle*. Used, carbon-dioxide filled blood comes into the right atrium. It moves into the ventricle and is pumped out to the lungs and skin, to be oxygenated. Clean, oxygenated blood comes from the lungs and skin into the left atrium. From there, it moves into the single ventricle, and is pumped out to the head and the body.

left atrium

right atrium

ventricle

Baby, it's cold outside!

Some frogs can become frogsicles and still live! The North American wood frog can withstand brutal winters. It can lower its body temperature to around 21°F, and then thaw out when the weather warms up. Its trick? The frog has an abundance of *glucose* (GLOO-kose), or sugar. Like antifreeze in a car's engine, glucose helps prevent water from freezing. These frogs can survive even when over half of the water in their bodies freezes solid!

what happens to food

Two unblinking frog's eyes—like twin submarine periscopes—extend from the pond's surface, searching the area. An unsuspecting mosquito buzzes low across the murky water—SNAP! In an instant, the insect is the frog's fast food. Insects, snails, spiders, worms, small fish, and even a live bat (like in the photo to the left). Nothing gets away from a hungry frog! Frogs only like to eat live prey. The bigger the frog, the bigger the prey. Large frogs even eat mice! With no real teeth to speak of, a frog must swallow its food whole.

Food to go, please!

Eating is fast business for most frogs. They flick out their tongues—with special glands to make them sticky—grab their prey, reel in their tongues, and swallow their supper! They do all this in less than one second. How's that for fast food? But what about frogs with no tongues, such as the South African clawed frog? They use their front toes to shovel food into their mouths. Talk about forced feeding!

South African Clawed Frog

Alimentary, Dear Watson

So the frog has its food, now what? A frog's digestion starts in its mouth, runs along the alimentary canal, and ends at the *cloaca* (klo-AY-kuh), where food waste is excreted. Digestive enzymes and chemicals are discharged into many parts of the canal—the mouth, the gullet, the esophagus, the stomach, the small intestine, the large intestine, the colon, the anus, and the cloaca. To begin breaking down the food, the stomach emits powerful HCl or *hydrochloric* (hi-dro-KLOR-ik) acid. This powerful acid is effectively neutralized before it enters the small intestine.

inside of mouth

alimentary canal

stomach

large intestine

cloaca

In one door, out the other

And then where does all the food stuff go? Digested food waste is passed into the large intestine and then the anus. The waste is then excreted into the cloaca—the chamber where all digestive debris leaves the bodies of amphibians, reptiles, birds, and some fish.

every breath you take

nares

Breathe in, breathe out... breathe in, breathe out. Animals, including humans, use *respiration*—or breathing—as a way to force oxygen into the cells of their body to live. Frogs are no different. They use their mouths or their nostril-like *nares* (NAR-eez) to suck in oxygen. As the oxygen travels into the frog's bloodstream, the heart then pumps it through the body. After the heart delivers oxygen-rich blood to its destination, it removes the carbon dioxide-tinged blood. These gases are forced out of the frog's mouth as it breathes out. Humans do this too. The frog breathes in and the process begins again.

Every breath you take (and sometimes four)

Frogs can breathe in four different ways:
- Through their skin
- Through special membranes in their mouths
- Through their mouths, nares, and lungs
- Through gills—tadpoles breathe with gills and some adult frogs keep their gills

Frogs breathe through their skin!

Adult frogs—unlike tadpoles—have lungs. They absorb a lot of oxygen through their skin. Few animals have such an efficient system! Some snakes also breathe this way. *Keratin* (KAIR-uh-tin) is the secret. Keratin is a protein found in hair, fur, scales, and skin. A frog only has keratin on its feet. Without keratin, liquids and gases can pass right through a frog's thin skin and into tiny blood vessels!

A frog's breathable skin.

no straws needed!

Frogs drink through their skin too!

Slippery when wet

Got moist skin? The down side of a frog's not having keratin means that it's hard to keep liquid *in*. If a frog's skin dries out, it's susceptible to skin infections and dehydration—which could lead to death. Glands in the skin moisten the frog's surface with slimy mucus. Moist skin is vital for absorbing oxygen and expelling carbon dioxide.

An open-and-shut case

Frogs actually swallow air! Like humans, a frog's lungs expand and contract. Frogs don't have a muscular diaphragm to pull the air in. Instead, air flows into the mouth and throat. The mouth closes, and strong muscles contract to force air into the lungs. With its mouth shut, the frog can suck air in through its nares using similar muscle contractions. This is a handy trick when it's lying in the water!

nares

One way frogs suck in air is through their nares.

Green submarine

When the need to float arises, frogs use their lungs. The frog inflates its lungs to float. To sink, it deflates them by breathing out. This is the same way a submarine rises and dives. Tadpoles use this lung technique to feed on the bottom of the pond, halfway up to the surface, or while they are on the water.

Hairy frogs?

Who ever heard of a hairy frog? Seriously, they do exist! Male frogs of one West African species grow hair-like skin projections on their bodies and legs during breeding season. These "hairs" greatly increase the surface area of the skin. This gives them a larger surface for absorbing oxygen. All that extra oxygen is a must for the hard work of breeding, and for staying underwater for long times to tend the fertilized eggs.

West African hairy frogs

a bundle of nerves

A frog's brain.

forebrain

cerebellum

spinal cord

It's not the brain, it's how you use it. Humans and frogs use their brains differently. In a human brain the cerebrum (suh-REE-brum)—the part devoted to thinking and judgment—is huge. Not so with a frog (probably why there aren't any famous frog philosophers). In a frog brain, the *cerebellum* (sair-uh-BELL-um)—the portion used to control the senses and actions like leaping, swimming, eating—is the largest part. The brain hooks to the bundle of nerves throughout the body and tells humans—and frogs—what to do.

Doing a "180" with their eyes

Bulging from the top of its head, a frog's eyes are almost all-seeing! A frog can see in front of itself, to its sides, and even part way *behind* itself! Frogs are great at sensing and seeing movement. They also have incredible night vision. These skills help them find their food more easily. Like other animals' eyes, frog and toad eyes have cone cells to help them see in color.

Red-Eyed tree frog

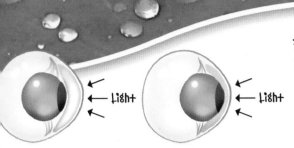

Frogs change their focus by moving the lenses of their eyes forward or backward instead of changing the shape of the lens.

They also have *two kinds* of rod cells, to aid their vision in low light. It is unknown how frogs use the "extra" type of rod cell. Humans and other mammals change the focus in our eyes by shifting the shape of the lens. Frogs change focus by moving the lenses forward or back.

Cool shades!

Frog irises come in a rainbow of colors—brown, bronze, silver, gold, red, and green. Their pupils come in many shapes: round, vertical slits, horizontal ovals, or heart, triangle, or even star shapes! Frogs that feed at night are more likely to have these unusual (and cool) pupils. These *nocturnal* feeders are more sensitive to light. These special pupil shapes react to light and close more quickly than regular round pupils.

Ear's the true story

Frogs don't seem to have ears! But look a bit closer. You'll see a round patch of skin supported by a circle of *cartilage* (car-TIL-age)—the type of tissue found in the tip of your nose. That's the frog's eardrum—also called the tympanic membrane. When sound waves hit the outside of the eardrum, the membrane vibrates. This vibration moves a small rodlike bone called the *columella* (kol-yuh-MEL-uh). The other end of the columella is attached to the fluid-filled inner ear. The motion of the columella makes the fluid move. That tickles about 1500 sensory hairs lining the inner ear. These hairs send signals to the brain—just like your ear!

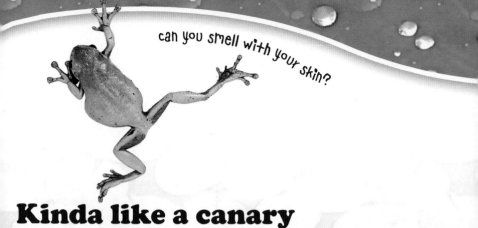

can you smell with your skin?

Kinda like a canary

Did you know that frogs smell with their skin? Smelling is basically just sensing molecules in the air around us. Frogs can sense the molecules that collect on their eyes and skin. This makes them very sensitive to the presence of dangerous chemicals. Frogs have been called "canary species." Like the canaries used by miners in coal mines, they are the first ones to be affected by "bad air."

In hot water

Stop us if you've heard this one: frogs will hop out of hot water, but won't leave if the water is heated up gradually. True or false? FALSE! Frogs can sense gradually heated water—and they're gone when it gets too hot!

You take the high note
Frogs sort sounds into two categories.
Higher-pitched sounds belong to other frogs and
lower-pitched sounds belong to predators.

Of all the nerves!

Proprioceptor (pro-pree-oh-SEP-der) organs are special nerve cells used by frogs and other animals. These nerve cells, found in muscles, tendons, ligaments, and joints, sense tension and stretching. The proprioceptor helps frogs know the position of their body parts. This helps their brains coordinate the complex muscle movements used in common frog movements like swimming and leaping.

the proprioceptor helps frogs know the position of their body parts.

boning up on bones

Your leg bone is connected to your pelvis bone... and so is a frog's. Humans and frogs share a similar skeleton. Like us, a frog's bones help to support the shape of the body. Also like human's, a frog's bones are essential for the muscles, tendons, and ligaments. The bones connect these body parts so that they can work together. Unlike humans, however, a frog's skeleton is perfectly designed for a frog's main way of getting around—jumping!

Nice bridge work

There are definitely bones about it! The frog's backbone is built of a chain of 10 hollow vertebrae. The last one of these is made of several vertebrae, which are fused together. These make up a unique structure called the *urostyle* (YER-uh-stile). Like the girders that hold up a bridge, the urostyle supports the frog's legs as it hops.

Soft or hard?

One thing that you can say about certain frogs—they are *not* all hard-headed! The skulls of most frogs are made of cartilage, rather than hardened bone. Most toads—and some frogs—have bony, or *ossified* skulls. They may also have ridge-like crests on their heads. Land-based frogs are more likely to have ossified skulls. This may help protect them from predators.

No teeth

Got teeth? Unlike humans, most frogs have no teeth on their lower jaws. The small, curved teeth around the edge of their upper jaws are called *maxillary* (MAX-ih-lair-ee) teeth. These help frogs hold onto prey as it is pulled into their mouths. A set of *vomerine* (VO-mer-rine) teeth can be found in the roof of some frogs' mouths. These "teeth" are used not for chewing but for helping get prey in the right place to be swallowed and to keep it from escaping.

glossary

Amphibia: Meaning "both lives," this is the zoological group of creatures who can breathe on dry land and in the water.

Amplexus (am-PLEK-suss): a male frog's arm and chest muscles grown during breeding season to ensure that he will be able to hold on tight to the female for hours at a time.

Antagonistic muscles: Muscle groups that contract as others extend.

Anurans: The amphibian group of frogs and toads.

Caecelians (si-SILL-yunz): Include blind, legless, wormlike animals.

Cartilage (car-TIL-age): The type of tissue found in the tip of your nose.

Cerebellum (sair-uh-BELL-um): This part regulates and coordinates the frog's movements—such as leaping, swimming, and eating— and senses.

Cerebrum (suh-REE-brum): The part of the brain devoted to thinking and judgment.

Chromatophores (kro-MAT-uh-forz): Special cells in a frog's skin that control the color.

Cloaca (klo-AY-kuh): An area at the end of a frog's alimentary canal, where food waste is excreted.

Columella (kol-yuh-MEL-uh): A small rodlike bone in the frog's inner ear.

Dendrobates: The most well-known of poison dart frogs.

Glucose (GLOO-kose): Sugar.

Hylidae: The family of tree frogs.

Keratin (KAIR-uh-tin): A protein found in hair, fur, scales, and skin. Frogs only have it in their feet.

Maxillary (MAX-ih-lair-ee) *teeth:* The small, curved teeth around the edge of a frog's upper jaw.

Melanophores (muh-LAN-uhforz): The largest and deepest layer of chromatophores.

Metabolize: To turn food into energy.

Nares (NAR-eez): Nostril-like membranes that help frogs breathe.

Nictitating membrane: It lowers to protect a frog's eyes.

Nocturnal: Active at night.

Nuptial (NUP-shul) *pads:* Where male frog's "hands" join their arms.

Oocytes (OH-uh-sites): Egg cells in female frog's ovaries.

Proprioceptor (pro-pree-oh-SEP-der) *organs:* Found in muscles, tendons, ligaments, and joints, these nerve cells sense tension and stretching.

Ranidae: The family of true frogs.

Respiration: The way animals force oxygen into the cells of their bodies, also called breathing.

Tympanic membranes: The frog's external eardrums.

Urodeles (YER-uh-deelz): Include salamanders and newts.

Vomerine (VO-mer-rine) *teeth:* found in the roof of some frogs' mouths, these teeth help frogs to get their prey in the right place to be swallowed.

amazing frog facts

they are what they eat

Some frogs secrete poisons they extract from plants they eat. These toxic chemicals can stun or kill an attacking predator. These poisonous frogs often have bright colors on their skin, as a warning to potential predators. The frogs remain toxic by eating toxic foods like plants. If the frog were to eat only non-toxic foods, it would no longer be poisonous.

Nuptial agreement

Male frogs have nuptial (NUP-shul) pads where their "hands" join their arms. These pads help them hold on tight during amplexus. Spines on the arms of some frogs serve the same purpose.

It's a bird, it's a plane— it's a frog!

Frogs can leap up to 20 times their body length!

Eyes on the prize

Frogs blink to help them swallow. Special muscles lower a frog's eyes into the skull. The eyes act like plungers to help push food down the frog's throat!

Is this clean?

Unlike human hearts, a frog's heart can't keep "dirty" blood separate from "oxygenated" blood very easily. The wall of the frog's ventricle has deep pockets to help separate the blood flowing in from the right atrium (the blood full of carbon dioxide) and the left atrium (the blood rich with oxygen). Our hearts have four chambers, so they can keep the two types apart.

Making the pace

A cluster of nerve cells in the frog's heart helps control its pumping rate. These "pacemaker" cells act on their own to regulate the heartbeat—even when the heart is removed from the body!

Surfing the web

Just like swim fins help us move through the water, webbed feet help some aquatic frogs swim. The frog's elongated fingers and toes help the webbing to work its best.

Glass frog

Frogs of "glass"

Glass frogs were named for their translucent skin. If you look at their bellies, you can actually see bones and internal organs... even the beating heart!

taking the red-eye flight!

If disturbed while sleeping, the red-eyed tree frog opens its bright crimson eyes to surprise and scare its predator. Before the predator knows what has happened, the frog makes its getaway.

Red-Eyed tree frog